MY FATHER'S PLAN

written by **Courtney Jo Warner** • illustrated by **Elyse Thompson**

CFI • An imprint of Cedar Fort, Inc. • Springville, Utah

Before the world was green and blue,
I lived in Heaven and you lived there too.

We lived as a family with Father and Mother,
and lots . . . and LOTS of sisters and brothers.

Yet, something was Missing. We weren't quite complete,
for we had no bodies that could smell, touch, or eat.

But no need to worry! Our Father's all knowing,
and he had a plan to help us start growing.

Letting us choose was part of God's plan,
and that's how the war in heaven began.

For we had one brother who said, "Listen here!
My plan is better, so lend me your ear."

"We should not choose between wrong or right.
We should be forced to be good day and night!"

But Father said, "No,
that isn't the way.
You'll never learn if you
can't choose to obey."

That brother is Satan and he was cast out
with all of his followers who shared in his doubt.

Now that Satan was gone, Father's plan could go on.
And with help from Big Brother, He created the Earth,
so we could come down and get bodies at birth.

And now here we are in this beautiful place.

Teaching our bodies to dance, jump, and race.

But that isn't all our bodies can do.
Every day we are trying to make good choices too.

It can be hard to do things like share.

Especially on days when I feel like a bear.

Lucky for us we have our Big Brother,
who showed us the way to love one another.

When He came to Earth, He traveled to towns,
teaching and healing. His love knew no bounds.

He is the central part of our Father's plan.
Because He suffered, bled, and died for each man.

His name is Jesus, and because of his love,
we can all return to our home up above.

This, my dear friends, is the plan of salvation.
And now that you know it, go tell the whole nation!

For Evelyn my Sister in Heaven
and my Princess on Earth.

– Courtney

Text © 2022 Courtney Jo Warner
Artwork © 2022 Elyse Thompson

ISBN 13: 978-1-4621-4221-7

Library of Congress Control Number: 2021950770

Published by CFI, an imprint of Cedar Fort, Inc.
2373 W. 700 S., Springville, UT 84663
Distributed by Cedar Fort, Inc., www.cedarfort.com

Cover and interior layout by Shawnda T. Craig
Cover design © 2022 Cedar Fort, Inc.

Printed in the United States of America

10 9 8 7 6 5 4 3 2 1

Printed on acid-free paper